CONFIDENT KIDS®

Guides for
Growing a
Healthy
Family

To my nephews,
Timothy and Mickey,
who are learning to grieve too soon

Books in the
"Guides for Growing a Healthy Family" Series

I Always, Always Have Choices
All My Feelings Are Okay
Let's Talk, Let's Listen Too
Going through Change Together

If you would like more information about starting a
Confident Kids® Support Group program in your
congregation or community, please write or call:

CONFIDENT KIDS®
P.O. Box 922
Yorba Linda, CA 92686-0922
(714) 528-6237

L. Winkelman

Going through Change Together

Help Your Kids Take the Steps with You

LINDA KONDRACKI

Fleming H. Revell
A Division of Baker Book House
Grand Rapids, Michigan 49516

© 1996 by The Recovery Partnership

Published by Fleming H. Revell
a division of Baker Book House Company
P.O. Box 6287, Grand Rapids, MI 49516-6287

Printed in the United States of America

Library of Congress Cataloging-in-Publication Data

Kondracki, Linda
    Going through change together : help your kids take the steps
with you / Linda Kondracki.
        p.   cm. — (Guides for growing a healthy family)
        ISBN 0-8007-5603-7
    1. Life change events. 2. Life change events—Religious aspects—
Christianity. 3. Adjustment (Psychology) 4. Adjustment (Psychology)—Religious aspects—Christianity. 5. Loss (Psychology) 6. Loss
(Psychology)—Religious aspects—Christianity. 7. Child rearing.
8. Child rearing—Religious aspects—Christianity. 9. Change (Psychology) I. Title. II. Series: Kondracki, Linda. Guides for growing a
healthy family.
BF637.L53K66 1996
155.9'3—dc20   96-20410

CONTENTS

How to Use This Book

Each chapter in this book contains three sections, each of which is a distinct resource. They are as follows:

1. **"Getting Ready"—Parents' Pages**
   Each chapter begins with a section for your own growth. Included in this section:

   ▸ teaching pages, containing the main point of the chapter written at an adult level
   ▸ reflection questions to help you personalize the material
   ▸ key verses and short Bible studies to help you connect with God and His Word

2. **"Talking Together"—Read-Along Pages**
   The middle section translates the main point of the chapter into language your elementary-age children will understand. Reading these pages together and talking about the questions will help you communicate valuable life skills information to your children. Included in this section:

   ▸ teaching pages, written for elementary-age children
   ▸ a short activity

▸ a summary or "remember" section, clearly stating the main point of the chapter

3. **"Growing Together"—Family Activities**
The final section is perhaps the most important one of all. Doing one or more of the suggested activities will not only reinforce the skill building but will also give you many occasions for bonding as a family. Included in this section are three kinds of family activities:

▸ *Building on God's Word.* Helps your family connect with God and His Word by memorizing key Bible verses and participating in short family Bible studies.

▸ *Conversation Starters.* These questions and activities will engage your family in significant conversations and sharing times.

▸ *Family Night Activities.* Choosing one or more of these activities will help your family enjoy a fun evening together and learn valuable skills at the same time. You will find instructions for a variety of things to do, including crafts, plays, cooking, and family outings.

INTRODUCTION

hanges. They are a constant part of our lives. Some changes are easy to get through and we don't think much about them. But others are more difficult and painful to face, and we find ourselves doing everything possible to avoid dealing with them. That is particularly true when the changes involved are unexpected and/or unwanted.

This book is about what to do when major changes happen in our lives and the lives of our children. I wrote it for several reasons:

▶ because of all the struggles I have had over the years learning to deal with the changes in my own life

▶ because of the many children I work with every week who are disoriented and hurting from the drastic changes in family life going on in our culture

▶ because of the many adults I know who are suffering today as a result of unresolved issues from changes that happened years before

In the six chapters of this book, you will learn that change is a natural, normal part of living in our world, and facing it openly is the first step in managing it in healthy ways. You will also learn that everyone goes through the same six-stage process when changes come, and you will find practical suggestions to help you get through each stage and move on.

My hope for you and your family is that as you work through this book, you will learn to get through the changes in your lives in healthy, growthful ways.

CHAPTER ONE

Nothing
Stays
the Same
Forever

PARENTS' PAGES

GETTING READY

Change Is a Part of Life

There is a time for everything, and a season for every
activity under heaven:

a time to be born and a time to die,
a time to plant and a time to uproot,
a time to kill and a time to heal,
a time to tear down and a time to build,
a time to weep and a time to laugh,
a time to mourn and a time to dance,
a time to scatter stones and a time to gather them,
a time to embrace and a time to refrain,
a time to search and a time to give up,
a time to keep and a time to throw away,
a time to tear and a time to mend,
a time to be silent and a time to speak,
a time to love and a time to hate,
a time for war and a time for peace.

Ecclesiastes 3:1–8

*T*hese verses from the Bible present beau-
tifully one of life's greatest truths: *Nothing
stays the same forever.* Change is a normal part
of life on this earth. But knowing that change is
a part of life and coping with it when it comes can be
two very different things. Even changes for the better
can feel threatening and scary. Consequently, human be-

ings will go to long lengths to resist change. Why? Two reasons come to mind:

1. *Change creates losses, and losses must be grieved.* Whenever things change, we lose something. We can lose tangible things, like treasured possessions and relationships, or intangible things, like hopes and dreams and a sense of security. Even happy changes involve some losses. When we lose something important to us, we experience emotional wounds that can be healed only by grieving them through. Since the grieving process is painful and can take a long time, we quite naturally resist the changes we know will precipitate the grief response.

2. *Change upsets our sense of security and order and causes us to adapt to new ways of living.* Human beings like predictability. We create our living and working environments just the way we want them. We set our schedules to bring order to our daily lives. We choose our relationships with people we believe (or at least hope) we can count on to be there for us over the long haul. Although too much predictability can cause boredom, by and large we gain security from knowing where things are, what will happen each day, and whom we can count on in life. Significant changes, such as death, divorce, change of a job, leaving home, or moving, disrupt our sense of order and security and force us to adapt to living in new ways.

Since changes—even big changes—are a normal part of life, we must learn to deal with them in healthy ways. If we are so afraid of the grief and adaptation required to deal with a change that we go to great lengths to avoid it, we are in serious danger of getting stuck in unhealthy and self-destructive behaviors. Examples would be the following:

▸ a spouse who stays in an abusive marriage rather than facing the changes involved in establishing a new way of life

▸ a young adult who avoids taking on the responsibilities of living in the adult world by never leaving home

▸ a worker who never reaches his or her full potential out of fear of the changes that would be brought about by a promotion

The reality of life is that nothing stays the same forever. Things change whether we want them to or not. Managing change effectively is a two-step process. Both steps are equally important and sequential.

Step 1: Say good-bye to the old. This is the work of grieving whatever we lost in the change. Saying good-bye means letting go *emotionally* as well as physically of past relationships, possessions, locations, and so forth. The only way to do that is to grieve the loss.

Step 2: Say hello to the new. This is the work of adapting to a new way of life. This can be particularly difficult if we are dealing with a change we did not want in the first place. Adapting to life without a person who has died, adjusting to life after a divorce, or fitting into a new neighborhood after a job transfer will involve a difficult time of transition.

The place in which many of us get stuck in dealing with change in healthy ways is that we do not take seriously the need to say good-bye before we can say hello. In fact, it may take some time before we can move through the grief stages and get to the place where we can emotionally say hello to our new way of life. Therefore, the next five chapters of this book will take you on a journey through the grief process. As you move through each one, you will be guided through the process of saying both *good-bye* and *hello* in the important changes of your life.

For Reflection

1. On the time line below, chart the most important changes that have occurred in your lifetime. Include changes, such as moving, entering high school, birth of siblings, deaths or significant illness of family members or close friends, divorces, entering and leaving college, marriage, and birth of children.

Birth

Your
present
age

2. Write a few sentences about each of the changes you identified above.
Significant losses I experienced: _____

_____

_____

_____

Ways I was forced to adapt: _____

_____

_____

_____

3. Of the losses noted above, are there any that you have *not* adequately grieved? If yes, describe how that loss is still affecting you today.

_____

_____

_____

4. Describe a change you are facing today. What do you need to do to say good-bye (losses to grieve)? To say hello (adaptations called for)?

_____

_____

_____

Building on
God's Word

Read through Ecclesiastes 3:1–14, thinking about the changes that have occurred throughout your lifetime. Take special note of the fact that nothing stays the same forever—*except for the works of God!* Since God knows the end from the beginning and has ordained the cycles of life, we can trust Him to be our guide through times of change. Bring any changes you are currently facing to Him right now, resting in the fact that wherever this change takes you, God is now, and will always be, with you in the midst of it.

Changes, Changes Everywhere!

Why did Grandpa have to die?

I don't want a new teacher! I want Mrs. Smith forever!

Can't we send the new baby back? He's too noisy and messy!

Things change all the time. There are all kinds of changes:

Big changes—like moving to a new house or a new state.

17 ▶

Little changes—like painting your bedroom
a different color.

Happy changes—like the last day of school!

Sad changes—like parents getting divorced
or someone dying.

Changes that are small or happy don't usually bother us very much. But when changes
happen that are really big or very sad, we can
sometimes have a hard time getting through
them. That's because *when things change, we
often lose something important to us.* When we
lose things important to us, we feel hurt and
sad. And feeling hurt and sad is what makes big
changes so hard to handle!

Let's meet two kids and find out how they
handle change. First, there's Rodney. Rodney's
parents are getting a divorce, which is one of
the biggest changes any kid ever has to handle!
Sometimes he feels like his whole life will never
be the same again.

Next, we meet Kacey. Kacey and her family
recently moved to a whole new state. She
misses her old friends and school and neigh-

borhood. She wishes every day that they could move back to their old home, where life felt more safe and secure.

Both Rodney and Kacey are learning a lot about what happens when things change. Right now, they are feeling hurt and sad because of the changes in their lives. But they're learning how to handle the changes in healthy ways. That's important for all of us to learn, since changes happen in everyone's life all the time. In the rest of the chapters of this book, we'll follow Rodney and Kacey and see what they are discovering about changes—and what you can learn from them about handling the changes in your own life.

You may not realize it but you are probably facing lots of changes too. Use the space below to make a list of all the changes in your life.

Were you surprised to discover how many changes are happening in your life right now? Here's a story about a girl who never thought much about changes until she had to say good-bye to an old friend.

Good-bye, Georgie!

Melanie sat on the sofa staring in the shoe box. Oh, Georgie! How could you do this to me? she said softly. How could you die and leave me all alone? You were just about my best friend in the whole world. I told you some stuff I never told *anybody* else! Who am I going to tell my deepest, darkest secrets to now that you re gone?

Hey, Melanie, have you seen my . . . Melanie s brother, Joshua, burst into the room, looking for his baseball. He stopped short when he noticed his sister staring into the shoe box. Are you still holding that dead mouse? Why don t you just bury that thing before it starts to stink?

Melanie was horri ed. Don t talk about Georgie like that! He s a better friend to me than *you* will ever be!

Was a better friend, Mel. He s *dead*, remember?

Melanie looked into the shoe box and said sadly, He can t be dead, Josh. I need him. Who will I tell my secrets to now?

You can tell *me* your deep, dark secrets, sister dear!

Get a real thought, Joshua! I wouldn t tell you . . .

Yeah, okay. So get another dumb mouse to talk to. I think I saw one in the kitchen about a week ago!

I DON T WANT ANOTHER MOUSE! I WANT GEORGIE! Melanie wailed at the top of her voice.

Well, you can t have him, Mel. He s dead. Pew! I think I smell him starting to stink already! Josh pinched his nose and ran around the living room. Say good-bye and bury that thing!

Melanie ignored her brother s teasing and said seriously, It s just that I thought I d always have Georgie around to talk to. How can I say good-bye?

Josh shouldered his baseball bat and headed out the door. Well, little sister, that s life. Nothin stays the same forever.

Melanie sat still for a few moments. Then she put the lid on the box. Hmph. Nothing stays the same forever! That s the *pits!* she said as she headed for the backyard.

Let's Talk about It

1. What did Josh mean when he said, "Nothing stays the same forever"?
2. Have you ever had something change that you didn't want to change? What was it? What feelings did you have at the time?

Remember . . .

Nothing stays the same forever! Changes will happen throughout your life. But remember, too, that God is in charge of your life and will help you through times of change: "He has made everything beautiful in its time" (Ecclesiastes 3:11).

Growing Together

BUILDING ON GOD'S WORD

Ecclesiastes 3 Mural. In advance, prepare a 3- or 4-foot-long piece of butcher paper or shelf paper. Lay this out on a table or tape it to a wall so family members can work on it easily. Have available water-based markers or crayons, magazines with plenty of colorful pictures, scissors, and glue. Begin by talking about the fact that God has planned for change to be a part of life. Read Ecclesiastes 3 together, involving kids in the reading. Use your mural to make a contemporary version of Ecclesiastes 3. Ask, "What changes do we experience in our lives?" Put the answers in the language of Ecclesiastes 3 and add it to the mural. Examples:

A time for school . . . a time to be out of school.

A time for our family to have two children . . . a time for three.

A time to move into a house . . . a time to move out of a house.

When your mural has as many changes on it as you want, illustrate it with pictures and words you draw yourselves and/or cut out of magazines. End with a prayer time, thanking God for being with you through past

Growing Together

changes and asking Him to guide you through present and future ones.

CONVERSATION STARTERS

Stress Survey. Talk with your children about the fact that change is stress producing, and that it is normal to feel strong emotions when things change. It is also normal for people to react differently to changes. Ask each family member to respond to the statements below by choosing one of the following responses.

I would feel okay. ☺   I would be upset. ☹

I would be *very* upset. ☹   I wouldn't care. 😐

If I had to get braces (or glasses), I would . . .

If Grandma (or fill in any person or pet's name) died, I would . . .

If Mom and Dad got a divorce (or got back together), I would . . .

If I never had to go to school (or work) again, I would . . .

If I got a new stepparent, I would . . .

If the end of the school year were tomorrow, I would . . .

If I could live in another country for a year, I would . . .

FAMILY ACTIVITIES

Growing Together

If we had a new baby at our house, I would . . .
(Ask family members to add statements of their own.)

FAMILY NIGHT ACTIVITIES

Family Photo Album Night. Set aside an evening to talk about past changes in your lives by looking through family snapshots, slides, movies, and videos. Pay particular attention to the losses that occurred and the ways your family found to adapt to new circumstances. Ask questions like, "How did our family change when we moved to Dallas?" ". . . after Joshua was born?" ". . . when your dad got remarried?" You can also discuss developmental changes. "How are things different now that you are in junior high school?" "Do you ever wish you were little again, like you were in this picture?" Be sure to include lots of time for laughter and celebrating past good times, as well as moments of sadness over significant losses. End the evening by celebrating your present relationships with a trip to your favorite ice cream store or making your favorite family treat together.

Denial:
This *Can't* Be
Happening
to Me!

GETTING READY

An Emotional Dizzy Spell

"Look, Mom," three-year-old Mickey said as they drove into the garage, "Daddy's home. The Jeep's here." He leapt from the car and ran into the house. "See," he continued once inside. "I told you Daddy was here!" His mom's heart sank as she watched her small son. There was no Jeep in the garage and no Daddy in the house. Three weeks earlier, Daddy had moved out of the house and started divorce proceedings. Mickey was experiencing the first stage of the grieving process—denial. Being only three, his way of experiencing it was to fantasize that Daddy was still home.

When something changes in our lives, particularly if it is an unexpected or unwanted change, the first reaction we will have is one of shock. In this initial stage of facing the change, "I can't believe this is happening" is perhaps more appropriately stated, "I *won't* believe this is happening." There is a good reason for this: Denial is a form of emotional protection.

Whenever we feel threatened or endangered in some way, we automatically do what is necessary to protect ourselves. If we are going out in twenty-five-degrees-below-zero weather, we wear lots of heavy clothing; if we are going to take a pan out of the oven, we use an oven mitt;

if we are going to play football, we put on shoulder pads and a helmet; and if we are feeling dizzy we sit down and put our head between our knees to keep from passing out. In the same way, when we experience something emotionally painful and/or threatening, it can feel like an emotional dizzy spell. The first thing we do is "put our head between our knees to keep from passing out"—in other words, we go into denial. Denial is an emotional buffer zone that gives us time to gather our resources and find the strength to deal with whatever lies ahead. This is a normal and important part of the grieving process.

Everyone experiences denial when facing significant changes in their lives, but not everyone expresses it in the same way. Denial may be experienced in any of the following ways:

▸ "checking out" (emotional numbness that impedes normal functioning)
▸ sleeping excessively
▸ fantasizing or pretending the change didn't happen or is not permanent
▸ using alcohol, drugs, or food to avoid the pain
▸ directing feelings of anger, sadness, and so forth toward people or circumstances that have nothing to do with the change itself (this is called displacement)

This is certainly not an exhaustive list. Actually, any behavior that helps us avoid facing what is actually happening is a form of denial. Although denial itself is a normal and necessary reaction, there is a danger here. As you can see from the list above, many forms of denial are self-destructive. It is possible to get stuck in the self-destructive actions of denial and never move on to the other levels of grieving and adapting to a new way of life. Instead, we make the self-destructive behaviors our ongoing lifestyle—we become addicted to drugs and alcohol or let our displaced anger become a barrier that cuts us off from other relationships.

Using denial inappropriately is like keeping a bandage tight against a physical wound so that it never has a chance to heal. Bandages are necessary for a time, but at some point the bandage must come off and the wound be exposed to the healing properties of air. In the same way, at some point we must uncover our emotional wounds by coming out of denial and facing the change that has happened in our lives.

Remember—denial is an important part of the grieving process and it is important to allow ourselves and others a time for gathering the emotional resources needed to deal with the change. It is healthy as long as we do not get stuck there. So how do we come out of denial? Most of the time it will happen quite naturally. When we have gathered the necessary emotional resources, we will find ourselves beginning to talk about the change openly and honestly with others. *Letting others see our pain and asking for help* is the signal that we are moving out of denial and into the next stages of grieving.

For Reflection

1. How were changes handled in your home when you were growing up?
   - ☐ They were resisted at all costs; things changed very little in our family.
   - ☐ They were taken as a matter of course; things changed frequently in our family.
   - ☐ We never talked about what was happening; we were expected to just "get used to it."
   - ☐ We worked together to grieve and adapt to the new way of life.
   - ☐ Other: _____

2. What denial behaviors do you remember from your growing up years?
   Behaviors your parents used: _____
   Behaviors you used: _____
   Other: _____

3. Identify a recent time you used denial. Describe the behaviors you used and any correlation you see with what you learned in your family of origin.

   _____
   _____
   _____
   _____
   _____

4. Think about your family members today, particularly your children. Which statement would be most true of each one?
   - ☐ Uses denial when necessary but can move on when ready.
   - ☐ Denies feelings to the max!
   - ☐ Other: _____

Building on God's Word

A normal reaction when we are in denial is a disruption of our desire or ability to pray. Sometimes this leads to further distress because we feel guilty about not praying, cut off from God, or confused about God at a time when we need Him most. In those times, we can rest on the assurance of the following verses.

In the same way, the Spirit helps us in our weakness. We do not know what we ought to pray, but the Spirit himself intercedes for us with groans that words cannot express. And he who searches our hearts knows the mind of the Spirit, because the Spirit intercedes for the saints in accordance with God's will.

Romans 8:26–27

PARENTS' PAGES

If you are stinging from a painful time in your life and cannot seem to connect with God in prayer right now, remember that the Holy Spirit is holding you up to God and praying on your behalf. Ask God to help you rest in this promise and give you a special reminder today of His continued presence and love for you—even in the midst of this change.

No Way! Not Me!

When something changes that we don't want to change, the first reaction we have is to *deny* it, or pretend that it isn't happening. Denial is a way of protecting ourselves from the hurt we feel. Whenever we feel something is hurting us, or could hurt us, we do something to protect ourselves. What would you do to protect yourself in each of these situations:

▸ It's twenty-five degrees below zero outside and you want to go out and play.

- You are in the park and you think a man might be following you.
- You start to take a pan of soup off the stove and notice the burner is still on.
- Your best friend just tells you he or she is going to move away.

In the last case, you might have had a little harder time thinking about what you would do to protect yourself. Since the hurt you would feel is an inside or emotional hurt, you would probably use denial to protect yourself from the hurt.

There are many things we can do to protect ourselves from feeling hurt. We can pretend something isn't really happening. We can refuse to talk about it. We can sleep too much or eat too much. We can get really mad at *everybody,* and when they say, "What's wrong with you?" we say, "Nothing!"

Remember Rodney and Kacey? Let's see how they used denial when they first learned of the big changes about to happen in their lives.

Read · Along Pages

> Rodney and his parents are sitting at a table, all feeling very sad. Mom says, "Rodney, we have something sad to tell you."
>
> Dad says, "We're getting a divorce. I'm moving away today . . ."
>
> Rodney jumps up from the table, very upset. "I don't believe it!" he shouts. "It's not true! I won't listen to this!"
>
> Mom calls after him as he walks away, "Come back! We need to talk . . ."

Draw Rodney and his parents. What are the expressions on their faces?

Kacey and her mom are sitting together, and Mom is hanging up the phone. Kacey looks at her with anticipation and asks, "What did Dad say, Mom?"

"He got the new job, Kacey," Mom answers. "We'll be moving to Texas in a few weeks."

Kacey walks away, smiling. "Well, you and Dad can go, but not me!" she says. "No way, Mom. I'm staying here with my friends."

Draw Kacey and her mother. What are the expressions on their faces?

It's okay to use denial to protect ourselves. Denial gives us time to get used to the idea that something has changed, and to get ready to face all the things that will come next. However, the

danger is that we will get stuck in denial and end up hurting ourselves more than helping ourselves.

How do we *not* get stuck in denial? Take a look at Rodney and Kacey again. One of them found a healthy way to come out of denial and the other is still using denial to cover his or her feelings. Can you tell which one is still in denial?

> Rodney is sitting with his grandmother, who is comforting him. He says, "Nanna, I'm really scared about the divorce. What's going to happen to us now?"

Draw Rodney and his grandmother. What are the expressions on their faces?

> Kacey is hitting another girl on the playground. A teacher sees it and says,

> "Kacey! Are you fighting *again?* Report to Mr. Peabody's office—NOW!"

Draw Kacey, her classmate, and the teacher on the playground. What are the expressions on their faces?

If you said Kacey is still in denial, you're right! Rodney discovered the secret to coming out of denial. You can discover it too, by breaking the secret code. Here's a clue: A=1, B=2, C=3, etc.

$$\frac{\quad}{4} \ \frac{\quad}{15} \ \frac{\quad}{14} \ \frac{\quad}{20}, \quad \frac{\quad}{19} \ \frac{\quad}{20} \ \frac{\quad}{1} \ \frac{\quad}{25}$$

$$\frac{\quad}{19} \ \frac{\quad}{20} \ \frac{\quad}{21} \ \frac{\quad}{3} \ \frac{\quad}{11} \ \frac{\quad}{9} \ \frac{\quad}{14}$$

$$\frac{\quad}{4} \ \frac{\quad}{5} \ \frac{\quad}{14} \ \frac{\quad}{9} \ \frac{\quad}{1} \ \frac{\quad}{12}; \quad \frac{\quad}{20} \ \frac{\quad}{1} \ \frac{\quad}{12} \ \frac{\quad}{11}$$

$$\overline{1} \quad \overline{2} \quad \overline{15} \quad \overline{21} \quad \overline{20} \qquad \overline{25} \quad \overline{15} \quad \overline{21} \quad \overline{18}$$

$$\overline{6} \quad \overline{5} \quad \overline{5} \quad \overline{12} \quad \overline{9} \quad \overline{14} \quad \overline{7} \quad \overline{19}!$$

Dealing with changes and being in denial is nothing new. Here's a story from the Bible about someone who faced many changes in his life. Can you see how he used denial?

Well, Well, Joseph!

Joseph, my *dear* brother, come here. We want to *talk* to you. Come on, boys, let s get him!

Hey, guys! What are you doing? Let go of me! Is this a joke, or what? Give me my coat back! No! I don t want to go down into this welllll . . . !

I ll never forget that day! I landed with a thump in the bottom of a dry well out in the middle of absolutely nowhere dropped in by my very own brothers! I kept looking up, sure this was all a cruel joke and they would lift me out and we d all go home. I heard them laughing as they walked back to their camp re. Hey! I screamed. Heyyyyyy! You can t leave me here! Help me, somebody, please!

The only response I got was the sound of my brothers laughter, and then silence. By nightfall, I was very thirsty and very frightened. I could die down here didn t they know that? But they did know that that was the whole point. My brothers, my very own brothers, wanted to *kill* me. But why? Was it something I said? I thought back over my life . . . maybe it was the coat . . .

Joseph, come here. I have something for you, my father had called one day. He was carrying the most beautiful coat I d ever seen. It was long and woven with many colors not just the boring brown and tan we usually wore every day. This was the kind of coat every boy dreamed of owning but only a very few ever did. It was extravagant, that was for sure!

When I took it, my father said, Now remember, Joseph, you must keep this between us. Don t tell your brothers. I only have one coat, and I m giving it to you, my favorite son.

Sure, Dad! No problem! I said, glowing in the words my favorite son! I ran off to nd my brothers.

Look, guys, I said, strutting around in front of them like a peacock in full bloom. Isn t it beautiful? Dad gave it to me and said it was because I was his *favorite* son! Pretty neat, huh?

I did notice my brothers were sort of mad about that. But could I help it if I was our father s favorite son? That didn t seem to me like anything to want to kill me over!

I thought back some more, and remembered the time I had the dreams . . .

Hey, guess what? I mumbled through my breakfast cereal one morning. I had another dream last night. Want to hear it? As I think back now, my brothers didn t exactly jump up and down with anticipation. Instead, they all rolled their eyes and stared into their bowls. Simeon even said out loud, No! We

don t want to hear about your dream!
Didn t matter, though. I told them anyway.

I dreamed there were eleven stars and
the sun and the moon and they all came
over and bowed down to one star mine!
You know what that means, don t you? At
that, all my brothers looked at me and
started yelling.

You think we re all going to bow down to
you! Ha! No way, little brother!

Just because you re Father s favorite
doesn t mean a thing to us! He worships
you already, but as far as we re concerned
you re nothing, Joseph!

Bow down to *you!* That ll be the day!

Sigh. Looking back, I could see that my
brothers had hated me enough to throw me
in a pit and leave me for a long time to die.
I just didn t see it before. I was in *denial*
and told myself that no matter what they
said or did, brothers couldn t hate each
other, no matter what. Well, sitting in the
dark out in the desert knowing I could die
in the next few days was enough to bring
me out of denial. I never felt so alone and

frightened in my life. All I could do in that hole was ask God to be with me.

Hey! Boy, are you there? I looked up and saw a rope being lowered, but I didn t recognize the voice. Come on, grab hold. You belong to us, now! the voice said. I didn t like the voice and considered ignoring this person and waiting for someone else to rescue me. But then, there might not ever be anyone else, so I grabbed the rope and climbed out. When I got to the top, I found out that my loving brothers had cut a deal with a passing caravan of Ishmaelites. They were on their way to Egypt and my loving brothers *sold* me to them. They intended to sell me as a slave in Egypt. That was the Ishmaelites, all right anything for a buck! They tied my hands and set me on a camel. You should thank your brothers for this, they said. If it weren t for us, by this time tomorrow you d be buzzard meat!

They were right, of course. But inside I swore at my brothers and raised my voice to God. Why *me*? I asked. What will become of me now?

To be continued . . .

Remember ...

It's okay to be in denial for a time—it's not okay to get stuck there!

Remember too that no matter how you may be feeling, God still loves you and cares about you. Use these verses from the Bible to remind you that no matter how much things change in your life, the one thing that will never change is God's love and care for you.

Yes, I am sure that nothing can separate us from the love God has for us. Not death, not life, not angels, not ruling spirits, nothing now, nothing in the future, no powers, nothing above us, nothing below us, or anything else in the whole world will ever be able to separate us from the love of God that is in Christ Jesus our Lord.

Romans 8:38–39 ICB

Growing Together

BUILDING ON GOD'S WORD

Meet Joseph. Throughout the rest of the book, you will be following Joseph's story and the many changes he faced in his life. As you follow his story, you will see how all the stages of grieving relate to his experiences, and more important, how God was very much involved in his life—even through the times he didn't understand what was happening to him.

Read the story (found at the end of the last Talking Together section) to your children or, if you prefer to read it directly from the Bible, read Genesis 37. Then talk about the following questions.

1. Why were Joseph's brothers upset with him? (He was his father's favorite son out of all twelve sons.)
2. How did Joseph use denial? (He wouldn't believe his brothers hated him, even though they had given him several clear signs that they did.)
3. When did Joseph come out of denial? (When his brothers tried to kill him.)
4. One way we come out of denial is to tell our feelings to someone. To whom did Joseph tell his feelings? (God, when he was in the well.)
5. Did God care about Joseph when he was going through all this? (Yes; even though Joseph didn't un-

FAMILY ACTIVITIES

Growing Together

derstand what was happening to him at the time, God never stopped taking care of him. He had a special plan for Joseph, as we'll see in later chapters.)

End with a short prayer time, thanking God that nothing that happens to us will ever stop Him from loving and caring for us.

CONVERSATION STARTERS

"When I'm in Denial I..." Looking back over the various denial behaviors described in this chapter, ask each family member to describe what he or she does when in denial. To help you focus, think back over the changes you identified when you were looking through the family pictures. Then ask members to think of specific ways they used denial during those times. For example: "How did I use denial when Carrie was born?" or, "What did I do to handle my feelings when we moved here from Boston?"

FAMILY NIGHT ACTIVITIES

Play a Hiding Game. Playing together is one of the most powerful, *and most neglected*, ways of building relationships with your children. Particularly during times

▶ 46

Growing Together

of change and grieving, play may seem to be the farthest thing from your mind. But taking time out to play together may be one of the most important things you can do.

Spend an evening playing games with your kids. Since denial is a form of hiding, one option is to play hiding games. Let your kids choose the hiding games they know, or use the following ideas.

Treasure Hunt. Hide pieces of your favorite family treat around the house or yard. Turn family members loose to find them. Add variety by hiding half the supply first. Once that's found, let the kids hide the other half and the parents take a turn searching! When all is found—enjoy!

Sardines. This is a variation of hide-and-seek, only this time the person who is "it" finds a hiding place and all the other players go looking for him or her. As "it" is found, the players join him or her in the hiding place, squeezing together like sardines. Be prepared for lots of giggles as the hiding place gets fuller and fuller. When all have found the place, start a new round.

Anger:
It's Just
Not *Fair!*

GETTING READY

Why Am I So Mad?

*I*t was the first night of a new unit in our Confident Kids Support Group program. About fifty children in grades one through six were meeting in small groups to learn about feelings and to talk about their life experiences. I was conducting the parents' group in the room right next to the first- and second-graders. About halfway through the meeting, I heard the door of that room open and a crying child (with a Confident Kids facilitator) tumble out. The child was sobbing—loudly. Immediately, all conversation in our group stopped as each parent listened to see if the crying sounded familiar. One mother, who couldn't take the suspense any longer, went to the door and peeked out. "It's a little blonde-headed girl," she told us, obviously relieved it wasn't her child.

Then I watched as the woman sitting next to me closed her eyes and whispered, "Oh no!" She held tightly to her chair and said, "I knew this was going to happen tonight, but I'm not going out there. I'll let the facilitator handle it. After all, this is exactly why I brought my girls here, so they could have a place to talk. So much has happened to them in the past year, but I can't get them to talk to me about it. I know there must be a lot going on inside of them, but they act as though there isn't anything wrong at all." She went on to share with us her story of the many changes happening in their lives, and the way her first- and second-grade girls were handling it.

For the rest of the meeting we talked together about the grief process involved in handling changes. The immediate response to change—even in young children—is denial. As we learned in the last chapter, denial plays an important role in helping us prepare to face the change. At some point, however, there needs to be a break through the denial and an embracing of what has happened. That's what was happening with this little girl. Something that happened that evening crumbled the walls of her denial, and she began to move on.

After the meeting I learned the details of what had happened. "She was doing just fine," her facilitator shared with me. "And then during the prayer time, she said she wanted us to pray for her daddy. That's when she started sobbing. I took her out in the hall and sat with her while she said over and over, 'I miss my daddy! I miss my daddy!'"

The next morning I talked with her mother on the phone. "You know," she said, "last night she finally told me what happened in the group and we were able to talk about her dad. But there is something I don't understand. This morning when she got up, she was so angry! I don't know what her anger was about, and when I asked her, she didn't know either."

I knew. Her anger was a further confirmation that the denial had been broken and she was moving on—right into anger. For her, as for any of us, when we finally face a change head-on and realize it isn't going to go away, we *will* feel anger.

The stage of anger is perhaps the most difficult one for us to deal with because anger in and of itself is a difficult emotion for most of us to handle. But as with all the stages of grief, anger is an important part of the process. A change—particularly an unwanted change—creates strong emotional energy inside of us that must be released in some way. The purpose of anger is to allow us to vent that emotional energy. The familiar illustration of keeping a lid on a pot of boiling water helps us to understand the nature of anger. We can try to keep a pot of boiling water tightly covered so no steam escapes. But no matter how hard we try to keep the lid on, the steam will win in the end and blow the lid off. But when we vent the pot by tipping the lid, the steam can escape naturally and safely.

That's how anger works. When we feel it, we have two choices. We can pay attention to it and use it to help us move on in the grieving process or we can ignore it and let it find its own way out—most likely in hurtful or destructive ways. The one thing we cannot do is wish it away. It *will* win in the end.

So, how do we express our anger in healthy ways? Here are a few keys:

1. *Place the anger where it belongs.* Misplaced anger is the most common destructive way that anger is expressed.

If I am angry at my boss for taking my job away, I may express my anger to my children. I place the anger where it belongs by naming the source of the anger: "I am angry at my boss for taking my job away."

2. *Find an appropriate way to express the anger.* There are lots of healthy ways to vent strong emotions, such as anger. Here is a simple rule to guide you: Express your anger any way that works for you, *as long as* it is not destructive to yourself, another person, or property. Effective ways include writing, drawing, physical exercise, and talking about it in a safe place.

3. *Plan confrontations carefully.* If you are angry at another person, it is best to deal with your anger before confronting the other person so you don't find yourself saying or doing something you will regret. For example, you could write a letter to the person and wait until the anger has subsided before deciding whether to send it. There is certainly a place for confrontation. But by handling your anger first, you can be free to focus on the issues at hand, not the anger itself.

As with all the stages of the grieving process, we cannot heal completely until we get through this stage. That may take five minutes or five years. Just remember, it is okay to feel and express anger. But it is only by venting it in healthy ways that we can move on.

For Reflection

1. When you were growing up what did you learn about handling anger from the following?
   How your parents handled their own anger

   _____

   _____

   How your parents handled anger in the family setting _____

   _____

   How you were treated when you became angry

   _____

   _____

2. How do you handle anger today?
   ☐ I control it by stuffing it inside.
   ☐ I explode at anyone and everyone in my path.
   ☐ I change the subject or walk away whenever I feel it coming.
   ☐ I *never* get angry!
   ☐ I've learned to deal with my anger in healthy and positive ways.

3. What correlations do you see between questions 1 and 2? _____

   _____

   _____

What insights can you gain from your answers?

_____

_____

_____

4. What are you communicating to your children about handling anger in their lives?
I am helping them by _____

_____

I am hindering them by _____

_____

Building on God's Word

True or false: God's Word teaches us that being angry is wrong.

Many of us have grown up believing the answer to that question is *true.* This is usually based on a misunderstanding of this verse:

> In your anger do not sin.
> Ephesians 4:26

At first glance, this verse seems to say that we should not be angry. A closer look, however, reveals that the problem with anger is not *having* it, but what we *do* with it once we have it. God created anger, just as He created every other emotion we have. But of all our emotions, anger is one of the strongest and God is warning us that we can easily get caught in expressing it in destructive ways. Think about the following.

Do you avoid *anger* altogether, believing *it is a sin to be angry?*

Are there ways you sin (use destructive actions) when you are angry?

If you are dealing with angry feelings over an unwanted change in your life, bring your anger to God, expressing it as openly and completely as you can. Then ask Him to guide you to use your anger positively and keep you from expressing it in ways that are destructive to yourself or anyone around you.

I'm So Mad,
I Could Just . . .

Have you ever said those words? How did you finish them? "I'm so mad, I could just punch you in the nose!" Or maybe, "I'm so mad I don't ever want to speak to you again!" Or, "I'm so mad I'm going to smash this doll all to pieces!"

When we get *that* mad, we are feeling *anger*. Everyone feels angry sometimes. We can feel angry when something in our life changes, especially if we did not want the change in the first place. Feeling angry at those times is okay. However, what we *do* when we feel angry may

not be okay. Here's a good rule to follow when you feel angry:

> **I will express my angry feelings in ways that will not hurt myself, another person, or property.**

This is an important rule to follow because when we feel angry, we often want to do something that will hurt ourselves or someone else, or we want to break something. At those times, we need to stop and think of a better way to express our anger.

Both Rodney and Kacey felt angry about the changes in their lives. At first, they didn't know about expressing their anger in healthy ways. This is what they did instead.

Rodney is sitting at a table, feeling frustrated about his math homework and angry that his dad is not there to help. Mom stands behind him, looking concerned and sad. She says, "Can I help you with your math problems?"

> Rodney says, "No! It's Dad's job to help me with math and it's all your fault he's not here to do it!"

Draw Rodney and his mother. What are the expressions on their faces?

> Kacey is packing things in her room, looking very angry about the move. She is throwing something against the wall. Her little brother is trying to help. "Here, Kacey, pack this next," he says, handing her a teddy bear.
>
> "No!" Kacey yells. "I don't want to pack that now! Get out of here! You're just making a bigger mess!"

Draw Kacey and her little brother. What are the expressions on their faces?

Both Rodney and Kacey expressed their anger by hurting someone with their words, and Kacey broke one of her things when she threw it across the room. But there are lots of better ways of expressing anger that won't hurt anyone or break anything.

Look at the list of objects in the left-hand column on the next page. *Draw a line* between each one and the way (on the right) it could be used to express anger in healthy, nonhurtful ways. *Cross out* the words in the right-hand column that are hurtful ways of expressing your anger.

- pillow
- art supplies
- running shoes
- telephone
- box of tissues
- letter paper and envelopes
- punching bag

- write a letter to the person you're angry at
- kick your dog
- cry
- draw or paint how you feel
- get into a fight at school
- punch something that won't get hurt
- talk to someone about how you feel
- throw your toy truck through the patio door
- run around the block

Rodney and Kacey learned that it is okay to feel angry when things change but that they could choose better ways to express their anger. Here's what each of them chose to do.

Rodney is sitting at the table. His math book is closed and he is writing a letter to his dad. He writes, "Dear Dad, I need to tell you how I feel today . . ."

Draw Rodney writing his letter. What expression is on his face? What do you think the letter says?

Kacey is in the garage, punching a punching bag.

Draw Kacey. What expression is on her face?

Now let's take another look at Joseph and see how he got angry when a new change happened in his life.

It's Not Fair, God!

Egypt. That s where we ended up. A foreign country, and what a strange place! So many people! My family were shepherds and we lived in tents out in the country. But Egypt! Well, I d never seen anything like this before! How could I survive in this strange place?

Joseph, come here! The caravan leader had been talking furiously with an Egyptian man for a long time before he called me over. Well, well, he said, the gods must be smiling on you, Joseph. This man is Potiphar and he is a very important man in Egypt. He drives a hard bargain, but you belong to him now. Mind your manners and you ll do well. Otherwise . . . buzzard meat! Ha ha ha!

And then he was gone, and I was alone with this strange man in this strange place.

The gods smiling on me? Perhaps *forgotten* me was a better word!

Egypt. A strange place. But it didn t take me long to learn about it. My new master turned out to be a fair and honest man who was impressed with my curiosity about his country. In time, he made me head of his household a very beautiful home, indeed, I might add and I began to think that God had been with me after all. Life in this new place wasn t so bad. And then it happened.

Joseph, I heard from the other room. Come here, please, I need help with something. I was startled. I thought I was alone in the house. I felt a shiver go through me when I heard the voice. It was Potiphar s wife, and I didn t have a good feeling about this. She was, well, let s just say, a little strange. I ignored her call.

Joseph! How dare you ignore me! Come here, *slave boy!*

No sir. I didn t have a good feeling about this at all. I turned around to answer her call, and suddenly she was standing right in front of me. She had the funniest look on

her face, like she was up to no good. I
de nitely had a bad feeling about this!

Well, well, Joseph. We are alone in the
house. Why don t we just go into my
bedroom and see what kind of work needs
to be done there. I want you to keep me
company today. I m lonely.

I . . . I don t think that is a very good
idea. When your husband comes home
again I can see to the things in your room.
Until then, I ll just nish up out here.

How dare you disobey me? I could have
you sent away in a at minute! She could,
too, and I knew it! Now come on! she said
as she took hold of my cloak and started
pulling me along! This wasn t right, and I
wasn t going to do it. I prayed for help.

No, I said, I m going outside to attend
to matters there. Now please let go! Wrong
thing to say to this lady; I could see that
immediately. Her eyes ared with rage and
she grabbed on to my cloak even tighter. I
decided to make my exit fast! The only
way I could leave was to slip out of my
cloak. I glanced back over my shoulder as I
reached the door and saw her standing

there with it in her hand, looking very surprised!

That evening, when Potiphar called me into his of ce, I knew I was in trouble. My wife tells me you were bothering her today. She says you wanted to work in her bedroom and no matter how hard she tried to tell you to stay out, you insisted. And don t try to deny it; I found this on the oor. He had my cloak in his hand. I was had and I knew it. I was a slave and she was his wife. Even if I told him my story and he wanted to believe it, he would have to believe his wife. That s the way it was. I said nothing.

Potiphar sighed, and I knew what was coming. I like you, Joseph, he said. But I can t have this kind of behavior in my house. The guards are on their way. I hope you enjoy your prison cell!

I didn t enjoy my prison cell at all. It was worse than being in the well! Just when I thought life was all together and I was enjoying it again, I found myself facing another change. I was alone, and scared, and this time I felt something new I was

angry! I shouldn t be here! I hadn t done anything wrong! She lied!

Is this what I get for doing the right thing? I prayed. God, where are you now? How could you let this happen to *me?*

To be continued . . .

Remember . . .

It's okay to feel angry when things change—it's not okay to express it by hurting yourself or someone else.

God teaches us exactly that in the Bible:

When you are angry, do not sin.
Ephesians 4:26 ICB

FAMILY ACTIVITIES

Growing Together

BUILDING ON GOD'S WORD

Talk about Joseph. With your family gathered together, read the story of Joseph in the Talking Together section or read it directly from the Bible in Genesis 39:1–20. Then discuss the following questions.

1. What change happened to Joseph in this story?
2. What was he angry about?
3. How did Joseph express his anger? (He talked to God about it; Joseph certainly was praying while in prison.)

"Expressing Anger" Graffiti Board. The purpose of a Graffiti Board is to provide a place for writing and drawing about a particular theme. In advance, prepare a long piece of paper (such as shelf paper) or a large piece of poster board by writing this heading across the top:

In your anger do not sin. Ephesians 4:26

Then draw a line down the center, dividing it into two parts. Using old magazines, newspaper headlines, and markers, create a collage depicting destructive ways to express anger on one side of the line and positive ways to express anger on the other. Older children and adults can

Growing Together

particularly get into this activity by adding drawings, poems, and so forth to the Graffiti Board.

CONVERSATION STARTERS

Watch TV Together. TV programs are filled with expressions of anger. Spend an evening watching your favorite programs together, taking note of the following questions. Talk about them with your kids during commercials and between shows.

1. Which characters expressed anger in some way? What were they angry about? Were any of them angry because something had changed in their lives?
2. Which characters used unhealthy or destructive means to express their anger? What did they do?
3. Which characters used healthy means to express their anger? What did they do?

FAMILY NIGHT ACTIVITIES

Assemble Feelings Boxes. A Feelings Box contains items family members can use to express their feelings in healthy ways. You can have one big box for all family

Growing Together

members to use, or each person can have his or her own. Keep the boxes in an easily accessible place, encouraging family members to use them whenever they need to express strong feelings—particularly anger.

Involve family members in decorating the boxes by covering them with paper and adding decorations, such as cut-out letters and pictures showing faces and feelings. Provide a variety of items to place inside the box, such as drawing paper, markers, paints, notebooks, stationery, pens, running shoes, tissues, a small punching ball, a list of trusted friends and family to call, and so on. Talk about the usefulness of each item for expressing feelings, particularly anger. Place all items in the family Feelings Box. If family members are making their own individual boxes, let them choose which items they feel would be most useful to them.

CHAPTER FOUR

Bargaining: Let's Make a Deal!

GETTING READY

I'll Find a Way!

*I*n a parents' group, a mother says, "I'm worried about my son. He keeps trying to find ways to get his dad to move back home. I've told him and told him that his dad won't do that, but he keeps trying anyway."

In a cancer support group, a couple shares, "We just keep thinking there must be some way to beat this. There must be a doctor somewhere who can help, or maybe they will find a miracle cure any day now. We've even been to three different churches to ask the elders to anoint and pray for Will. We just have to find a way!"

These people are all experiencing the bargaining stage of the grieving process. This is the point at which we try to do something about the change that has happened. It is our attempt to undo an unwanted change, or at least minimize its effects by manipulating some of the circumstances.

At first glance, bargaining may seem like a form of denial. Both involve the internal feeling of "I won't accept this change." There is a big difference between the two, however. In denial, we *pretend* the change is not really happening. In bargaining, we *accept* the change as real and are now trying everything in our power to do something about it. It is a vitally important stage for several reasons.

- We are no longer paralyzed, as we are when in denial.
- We are taking control of our circumstances by actively exploring options open to us.
- We learn which circumstances we actually have power to manipulate in our favor and which are beyond our control.

Bargaining can take several forms.

1. *Internal bargaining.* This has to do with what is going on inside of us. It is changing the way we think and the messages we tell ourselves to make ourselves feel better. Examples would be the following:

- If I change the way I am, like picking up after myself or being more considerate of her needs, she will come back.
- If I sweet-talk my boss, he will reconsider and give me my job back.
- If I hurt him as much as he hurt me, I know I'll feel better.

This is the first level of bargaining, and many times we never move beyond it; we never actually act on any of the options we create in our heads. Just going through the exercise of thinking of them helps us feel better.

2. *External bargaining.* There are many times in bargaining when we actually do things to make the change go away or minimize its effects. Examples would be these:

▸ I didn't get the promotion I wanted, so I try negotiating a change in my present job description, or begin getting my résumé in order.

▸ I am facing a divorce I do not want, so I try getting my partner to go to marriage counseling or I promise to make personality changes if he will stay.

3. *Spiritual bargaining.* During the bargaining stage, it is quite natural for us to cling to verses from the Bible that promise us that if we have enough faith, God will answer our prayers. We translate that to mean that if we pray hard enough and long enough God will give us what we want. After all, what better source to turn to in an impossible situation than an almighty, loving God? And if that doesn't work, we may offer deals in exchange for miracles: "If you just do something about my son's drug problem, I promise I'll teach Sunday school the rest of my life!"

As you can see, bargaining is a highly emotional—not necessarily a rational—reaction to a painful or difficult situation. Often friends or family members watching a loved one going through this stage become quite concerned about some of the distorted or wishful thinking that is taking place. This is not only normal, however, it is an important process to go through. That's because we may not be able to emotionally let go of something until we feel we have done everything in our power to at least try to get what we want. And we cannot get to the later stages of acceptance and hope until we can emotionally let go of whatever we lost when the change happened.

Finally, we must remember that sometimes we are successful at bargaining and sometimes we are not. Couples do get help and get back together again, job descriptions can be renegotiated, and God does work miracles. Other times, however, nothing we do will help and the divorce happens, people die, or God does not work a miracle no matter how hard we pray or believe. Regardless of the outcome, the lessons we learned in the bargaining stage about our own personal power and the skills needed to successfully navigate through a difficult change will remain and be helpful to us again when facing new changes in our lives.

For Reflection

1. Describe a past or present change in your life, particularly an unwanted change. _____

_____

_____

2. How did you use bargaining to try to undo the change or negotiate its effects internally (to make yourself *feel* better)? externally (what did you *do*)? spiritually (what did you *pray*)? _____

_____

_____

3. Observe your children as they face changes in their lives. How do they use bargaining to manage these changes? _____

_____

How does knowing that bargaining is a normal part of the grief process help you in dealing with these behaviors? _____

_____

Building on God's Word

When we are involved in a deeply emotional grief process, prayer can be difficult. There may be long periods of wondering why this change is happening to *me* and particularly why God is seemingly not acting in *my* behalf. After all, if God is a loving God, why would He let me go through this difficult time in the first place?

Holding on to the following two principles can help you get through this stage.

1. *It is okay to ask God for what you want, or think you want, at the time.* It is also okay to ask God *why* questions: "Why is this happening; why don't You do something?"

2. *No matter what happens, God is, ultimately, a loving God who can be trusted.* Make the following verses your own today.

Trust in the LORD with all your heart and lean not
   on your own understanding;
in all your ways acknowledge him, and he will make
   your paths straight.

Proverbs 3:5–6

Maybe I Can Make This Change Go Away!

Mom, I'll do the dishes for you if you'll change your mind and take me to see a movie tonight!

If I promise to do all the work so you'll never have to do anything, can we get a dog, please?

I'll play Star Crashers with you now if we can play Din-O-Blaster next.

Do you ever say things like these to your family and friends? This is called *bargaining,* and it is one of the ways we can get things we want.

Most people use bargaining a lot; in fact, it is an important life skill to know. If we never used bargaining, we'd be stuck always doing what someone else wanted us to do.

When it comes to handling changes in our lives, we use bargaining too. Bargaining happens when we say things like, "There must be something I can do to make things go back to the way they were before." Or if we know the change won't go away, we may say things like, "What can I do to make myself feel better?" Let's see how Rodney and Kacey used bargaining to deal with the changes in their lives.

> Rodney is using bargaining to try to make the change in his life go away. He's talking on the phone to his dad. He says, "Dad, if I promise to clean out the garage and wash the car every week and not fight with Careen anymore, ever—will you come home again?"

Draw Rodney talking on the phone.

Kacey is using bargaining to make her change easier to deal with. Kacey says to her parents, "If I do more chores and save up my money for a plane ticket, can I go back to visit my old friends in New York?"

Draw a picture of Kacey and her parents.

Bargaining is important because it helps us learn two important things about the change that has happened.

1. *We have choices.* If you think hard, you can probably find lots of ways to at least *try* to get what you want. Even if you can't have your first choice (like getting your parents to get back together if they are getting a divorce), you will find that you can do lots of things to make the change easier to get through.

2. *Sometimes we can make things happen the way we want, and sometimes we can't.* It's always okay to try things to get what you want. However, you must understand that no matter how much bargaining you do, some things are beyond your control. By bargaining—trying lots of different things—you will learn what things you can make happen, and what things you can't make happen. Let's see how Rodney and Kacey made out with their bargaining.

> Dad says to Rodney, "Look, son, my moving out was about your mom and me—not you. There is nothing you can do to change that. I'm sorry."

Draw Rodney's face.

Kacey's parents say, "If you will work hard at making new friends here in Texas, *we* will pay for you to go to New York for Easter vacation."

Draw Kacey's face.

Now let's look in on Joseph. In the last chapter, we left him sitting in prison and probably feeling angry because he didn't deserve to be there. Now let's see how Joseph used bargaining to try to get rid of this unwanted change in his life. Can you find his bargain in this story?

Joseph Cuts a Deal

Prison! What a disgusting place! It was dark and smelly and lonely! For a long while, all the company I had were crawly things beetles and mice and rats. At rst, I didn t know how I was ever going to get through this awful change! But then I began to think that maybe there was something I could do about all of this. Maybe, if God would help me, I could think of a way to get out of prison.

Now think, I said to Harvey the rat that came most often to my cell. How am I going to get out of this one? There has to be a way! Harvey and I thought about all kinds of things. Some of them seemed like good ideas at rst but were really way

beyond my control. Like breaking out. Bad idea. Being chased by the whole Egyptian army as a jailbreaker was not my idea of having fun! Or maybe I could just scream and scream until they got tired of listening to me, and they would let me out just to shut me up . . . or maybe they d break my jaw to shut me up! Another bad idea.

But then there were the good ideas. Finally, I decided to ask God to help me be as kind and pleasant as I could no easy task, considering how angry I was! You know, Joseph, I said to myself, if you show them what a great guy you are, maybe they ll let you out! Or at least make life a little easier for you here. And you know what? It worked! God gave me lots of help to be kind and helpful, and soon the warden of the prison started giving me special things to do. In time, he put me in charge of all the other prisoners. Acting in ways that honored God got me a lot further than if I had kept on being angry and mean because I had been wrongly treated. But I still didn t get

what I most wanted they didn t let me out.

Then one day, things changed and I found a way to get what I most wanted. One morning, as I was attending the prisoners, I noticed that two of them seemed especially sad. Hey, guys, I said as I brought them their breakfast, something wrong?

Well, yeah, I guess so, said the one who had been the cupbearer of the king, before old Pharaoh got mad at him and threw him in prison. It s just that I had a dream last night, and I know it means something but there is no one here to interpret its meaning for me.

Me, too, said the other man, who had been the baker for Pharaoh before ending up in prison.

Maybe I can help, I responded quickly. God has helped me know the meaning of dreams other times; maybe He will tell me the meaning of yours.

For the next hour or so we talked. I told them the meaning of their dreams. It was good news for the cupbearer in three days

he would go before Pharaoh and all would be forgiven and he would get back his old job of serving wine and other drinks to the king. I felt a stab of sadness when I heard the baker s dream, however. The meaning was clear in three days he, too, would stand before Pharaoh. But Pharaoh would not be so kind to him. I choked on the words as I told this man that he was going to die. Finally, I had to get on with my rounds.

Hey, I said to the cupbearer just as I was leaving. I did something for you, now I need you to do something for me. In three days, when you are serving wine to Pharaoh again, please tell him about me! Tell him how I don t deserve to be here and ask for my release. He will listen to you.

Sure, man! he said, cheerfully. I d be happy to do that! You got it!

I bounced along that morning, delivering the rest of the breakfast trays. Finally! I thought. Finally, I am going to get out of this place! In three days, the cupbearer will be free and he will speak to Pharaoh about

me and then I ll go free! In just three more days . . .

To be continued . . .

Remember . . .

It's okay to use bargaining to try to get what you want.

It's also okay to ask God to help you, and tell Him what you would like to have happen. But you can also trust God to do the right thing, even if He doesn't give you exactly what you asked for. Remember this promise from the Bible:

Trust the Lord with all your heart. Don't depend on your own understanding. Remember the Lord in everything you do. And he will give you success.

Proverbs 3:5–6 ICB

FAMILY ACTIVITIES

Growing Together

BUILDING ON GOD'S WORD

Talk about Joseph. With your family gathered together, read the story of Joseph in the Talking Together section or read it directly from the Bible in Genesis 39:20–40:22. Then discuss the following questions.

1. What did Joseph want more than anything else? (To get out of prison.)
2. What different things did he think of to do?
3. How did asking God to help make a difference? (God helped him be kind and helpful, even when he felt angry inside. Like the memory verse says, God gave him success.)
4. What can you ask God to do to help you with a change in your life?

Memorize Proverbs 3:5–6. Memorizing verses from the Bible is an excellent way to equip your children with biblical truths that can help them throughout their lives. These verses from Proverbs have been comforting to many Christians throughout the centuries. You can make a game of memorizing them by starting with one person who says the first word of the verse and having all family members take turns adding the next word until the whole verse has been said correctly. When someone

Growing Together

misses, start over. Continue until everyone can say the verse without help.

> Trust the Lord with all your heart. Don't depend on your own understanding. Remember the Lord in everything you do. And he will give you success.
>
> Proverbs 3:5–6 ICB

CONVERSATION STARTERS

Let's Make a Deal. You can practice the art of bargaining with your family. Choose an area of conflict, such as cleaning rooms, doing chores, or rules about TV time. Involve everyone in negotiating a position that all can agree to. Proceed by following these steps:

1. *Introduce the problem.* "Your room looks like a disaster area."
2. *Have each side state their position.* Child: "I like my room the way it is. I think I should keep my room any way I want." Parent: "I don't want you growing up living like a slob."
3. *Brainstorm possible solutions to the problem.* Remember, brainstorming is a collection of ideas with no judgment of any of them. Just generate a list, like this one:

Growing Together

Let Jimmy keep his room any way he wants.

Jimmy keeps his room the way Mom wants.

We hire a maid to clean Jimmy's room.

Jimmy cleans his room more often than he does now.

We set certain basic rules, like the bed must be made every day.

Jimmy will clean his room once a month—whether it needs it or not.

4. *Each side says what they need.* Jimmy: "I need my room to be my own place." Parent: "I need your room to look presentable and I need you to grow up learning what it means to properly take care of your things."

5. *Using the statements of need, sort through your list of options until you arrive on one or two that will satisfy both parties.* Remember, you are bargaining with each other to reach a common solution. That means both sides must respect the other's needs. Mom: "The maid idea is out, but I could be okay with you having your own private space, if you will agree to certain basic standards." Jimmy: "Okay, as long as I get to help say what they are."

Growing Together

FAMILY NIGHT ACTIVITIES

Let's Make a Deal Game. Before gathering your family together, prepare a number of packages for this game, one for each member of your family, plus a few extra to increase the drama of the game. Wrap the packages in such a way that the bigger and prettier ones contain things your kids would NOT like to get, such as a can of spinach, an onion, or an empty candy wrapper. As the packages get smaller and plainer, put more exciting things in them, such as a real candy bar or party-favor-type prizes. In the smallest box, wrapped with newspaper, place a dollar bill or something else your kids would really like.

To play the game, put all the packages in the middle of the table. Now make out slips of paper with numbers from one through the number of persons playing. Let everyone draw a slip from a hat or basket. The number on the slip determines the order in which they can choose a package from the pile. Starting with number one, let each choose a package. When all have chosen, but before opening them, talk about how happy they are with their choices:

> Would you rather have a different package? Why or why not?
>
> What basis did you use for making your choice? (Probably they chose on the basis of size and attractiveness.)

Growing Together

Now allow time for bargaining. Would anyone like to try
to get a different package? Allow all to try to get a different package, if they desire. They can use any means they
wish to make a change, except force. When all have settled
on the package they will keep, let everyone open his or her
package. Now talk about the contents of the packages.

Are you happy with what came in the package you
opened?

If you got the package you really wanted, were you
happy or disappointed when you opened it?

If you *didn't* get the package you wanted, did you feel
any different once you saw what was inside?

Was there any way you could have gotten more information to make a better choice, other than what the
outside of the package looked like?

End the game by pointing out that sometimes when we
are bargaining it is easy to think we know what we want
and try to get it any way we can. But in the end, the thing
we *think* we most want may not be what is best for us or
the other people involved. Sometimes all we can do is hold
on and wait to see how things will work out. (Example: A
new baby in the family can be a difficult change for kids.
But in the long run, having brothers and sisters is a good
thing!)

Depression:
It Hurts *So*
Much!

GETTING READY

Will I Ever Be Happy Again?

There comes a time in the grieving process when reality finally hits home and we realize this change is here to stay. The wave of anger has subsided and we have done all the bargaining we know how to do—but the change is still here. It is at this point when we feel the deepest sadness. As with all the other stages, this stage is also necessary to the grieving process—the deep sadness is the place where inner healing finally starts to take place.

But depression can feel frightening. It is characterized by a sense of hopelessness that feels as though we will never be happy again. We also experience a sense of isolation that says no one in the whole world has ever felt this before and a paralyzed feeling that inhibits our desire to do any of our normal activities. At times it can easily feel as though we will never come out of the sadness—that this is the way we will be for the rest of our lives!

I remember a time when I heard myself praying, "Dear God, where are You? I feel as though I'm in the middle of a huge house with no windows and no light and only one door—and You just slammed the door tight, locked it from the outside, and went away. And the hardest part of all is that I don't know if You're ever coming back."

What brought on such a desperate prayer? I had suffered five major losses in my life, beginning with the death of my father and continuing one after another in a little over a year's time. The weight of those losses finally caught up with me and I began to feel that not even God could help. It was a blackness I had never known before, and I felt very much alone.

Over the years since that time, I have discovered that my experience was not unique. Many people report similar feelings on entering the stage of depression in their own grief experiences.

It is that sense of isolation and paralyzation that makes getting through this stage difficult. But we can make it through if we think of it in terms of it being a kind of emotional intensive care, during which the wounds caused by the change in our life can take time to heal. And, just as physical intensive care involves giving our bodies what they need to recover from a physical injury, so there are things we can do for ourselves to facilitate our emotional healing. This is called self-care and includes the following:

1. *Answer the question "What do I need right now?"* Many of us grew up believing that it was not all right to be depressed or sad, and that we should be able to "snap out of it" and get on with our lives. So the first answer to this question may be to give ourselves permission to feel sad and take healing time. Beyond that, each of us must identify what will help us the most. For me personally, I usually need two things. First, I need to take time to journal as a way to keep my thoughts clear and provide an

outlet for my feelings. Second, I need to be careful to maintain some normal contact with friends so I don't give in to my propensity to isolate myself completely.

2. *Tell others what we need from them.* When we are in the stage of depression, our friends and loved ones feel at a loss to know what to do for us. For their sake as well as our own, it is important to give those closest to us clear messages about what we need from them. We may need to ask for extra time to just "dump our feelings" in a safe relationship. Or, we may need to ask friends to go shopping or play an extra round of golf. I usually have to tell my friends that I need extra time alone but I assure them that I'm okay. Or I may ask them to be with me without trying to cheer me up. The point is to be sure to let others know what *you* need so they will not be left wondering what to do for you, and you will be sure to get what you need from them during this time.

3. *Remember that the sadness will not last forever.* This may sound like a cliché, but it is important to keep reminding ourselves of its truth when we are in the midst of depression. This is another place where journaling is helpful to me; reading through past entries helps me recall other times when I felt as though things would never get better and remember that they always did. This gives me the assurance that this too will pass and life will be good again.

The sadness of depression is important to go through, but we must be cautioned that it is possible to get stuck there. Sometimes the sadness feels so great we are tempted to refuse to do any self-care at all, remaining totally isolated for long periods of time. Or we may become so accustomed to the feeling of sadness that we resist the good feelings when they begin to return. Most of the time, however, when the time is right and our inner healing is well on its way, we will find ourselves moving on in the process—right into acceptance and hope.

For Reflection

1. How was sadness or depression handled in your family of origin?
   - ☐ It was not allowed; we had to "put a smile on our faces" or "stop being a baby and grow up" no matter what happened.
   - ☐ Depression is a part of our family history; my mother/father was always depressed.
   - ☐ It was okay to be appropriately sad; I saw my parents cry when they were sad and laugh when things were good again.
2. When you are grieving deeply, what do you most want from others around you?
   I want my family to _____
   I want my friends to _____

   What do you need to do to take care of yourself?

3. Rate yourself on your ability to help your children through their times of grieving:

I try to take the sadness away by telling them to "put on a happy face."
□ Always □ Often □ Never

I ignore their sadness because it makes me uncomfortable.
□ Always □ Often □ Never

I assume that if they are out playing with their friends everything is okay.
□ Always □ Often □ Never

I encourage them to talk about their feelings and allow them to heal in their own time.
□ Always □ Often □ Never

Building on God's Word

The most difficult part of dealing with depression is the sense of isolation and aloneness that accompanies it. It can be a frightening feeling of being alone in the darkness, where even God is not present. If that is your experience today, open your Bible and read Psalm 139. This psalm gives powerful assurance of God's guiding hand in our lives, beginning before we were even born!

Pay particular attention to the verses printed here, letting them reassure you that no matter what has happened in your life, or how alone you may feel today, God is still with you every step of the way!

> If I say, "Surely the darkness will hide me
>   and the light become night around me,"
> even the darkness will not be dark to you;
>   the night will shine like the day,
>   for darkness is as light to you.
>
> Psalm 139:11–12

I'm So Sad

Can you remember a time when you felt really, really sad? Maybe it was when someone you loved died, or you moved far away from your very best friends. Can you remember how you felt during those times? Which of these describes it?

didn't want to eat
couldn't sleep very well—or maybe wanted to sleep too much
didn't want to play with anyone
just wanted everyone to leave you alone
cried a lot

All of these things can happen to us when we are going through a big change. This is called depression and it means feeling very, very sad. Let's take a look at Rodney and Kacey and see what happened to them when they started feeling depression.

Rodney is sitting on his bed looking sad. From outside the room his mom calls, "Rodney, telephone! Jeff wants to come over and play." Rodney thinks, *I don't want to play with anyone today.*

Draw Rodney sitting on his bed.

> Kacey and her parents are sitting at the dinner table. Kacey has her head in her hands and is not eating; she looks sad.
> Mom says, "Kacey, you haven't touched your dinner." Kacey responds, "I'm never going to eat again."

Draw Kacey talking to her mom.

It's okay to feel sad when things change in our lives; everyone does! But when it happens, you can help yourself get through it by doing two things.

1. *Remember that the sadness won't last forever!* Like Rodney and Kacey, when we feel depressed we usually feel like we will never, ever feel happy again. But that is not true. All

sadness goes away after a time. You can help yourself get through the sadness by telling yourself, "I feel sad today. But I won't feel sad forever. The sadness will go away and I will feel happy again." Sometimes it takes a long time for the sadness to go away, but it always does! Just remember, no matter how bad you feel, the sadness will *not* last forever!

2. *Tell others how you are feeling and what you need from them.* Many people try to pretend they are *not* feeling sad when they really are, but that only makes things worse. It is much better to be honest about your feelings and say, "I'm feeling sad and that's okay." You can also help yourself by thinking about what you would like other people to do for you. You might say something like this:

- I don't feel like playing anymore today. Will you call me tomorrow?
- Can I have some paper so I can write a letter to Susie and tell her how much I miss her?
- Mom, can I just sit next to you for awhile? I feel really sad today.

Telling others how we are feeling and what we need won't take the sadness away but it will make it easier to feel.

Now let's see how Rodney and Kacey handled their depression.

> Rodney is talking on the phone. He says, "I'm sorry I can't play, Jeff, but I miss my Dad a lot today. Call me tomorrow, okay?"

Draw Rodney's face as he talks on the phone.

> Kacey is sitting on her mom's lap. She says, "I miss my friends and our old house a lot!"
>
> Mom says, "I know, dear. It's okay to feel sad."

R e a d · A l o n g   P a g e s

Draw Kacey sitting in Mom's lap.

Now think about something that is making you feel sad today, or something that made you feel sad in the past. Can you make up a story about it? Draw your story in the boxes.

Now let's take a look at Joseph, and find out about a time he felt depressed too.

Did You Forget about Me Too, God?

Guard! I shouted as the first morning guard came into the prison courtyard. Any news for me today?

He looked back at me and shook his head. No, Joseph. No news today. Just like there wasn t any news yesterday, or the day before that, or the weeks and weeks before that! Don t you ever give up?

His words stung me inside as I watched him go about his duties. What went wrong? I ve asked myself that question about a zillion times over the past, well, almost a year now. The cupbearer promised he would speak to Pharaoh on my behalf. But I ve been waiting and waiting and waiting; and still no word from Pharaoh. Meanwhile, I m still sitting here in

this rotten jail for something I didn t do! I think I want to die.

I don t know what to do. I didn t want my life to be this way. It seems like everything that has happened to me has been the pits! I started out as the favorite of my father, and the next thing I know, I m sitting at the bottom of a pit, left to die by my own brothers! And then I m sold in a strange land to a strange man and his weird wife! But things were just starting to feel okay again, when *BAM!* I m accused of something I didn t do and hauled off to jail. Then I do a favor for a friend, and in return he promises to help me get out but he forgets all about me, and here I am!

But the worst part of all is that I don t understand You, God! How could You possibly love me and let me sit in this awful place for all these days and weeks and months and now a whole year! Have You forgotten about me too, God?

To be continued . . .

Remember . . .

You can take care of yourself when you feel sad by remembering that the sadness won't last forever and telling others what you need.

Remember, too, these verses from the Bible. They tell us that God is with us even when we feel alone and sad. He is still taking care of us no matter where we are or what has happened in our lives.

Where can I go from your Spirit?
   Where can I flee from your presence?
If I go up to the heavens, you are there;
   if I make my bed in the depths, . . .
even there your hand will guide me,
   your right hand will hold me fast.
                          Psalm 139:7–10

Growing Together

BUILDING ON GOD'S WORD

Talk about Joseph. With your family gathered together, read the story of Joseph in the Talking Together
section, or read it directly from the Bible in Genesis 40:23.
Then discuss the following questions:

1. What were the things that happened to Joseph that
   he was feeling depressed about? (His brothers
   wanted to kill him; he had to move to a strange place
   where he didn't want to be; he was accused of something he didn't do; he was being punished unjustly;
   the cupbearer broke his promise to help.)
2. What thoughts do you imagine Joseph had about
   God? (I wouldn't be surprised if he felt that if God
   really loved him He wouldn't let him sit in prison;
   therefore, even God had forgotten him.)
3. Think about the things Joseph was depressed about.
   Can you think of a time you experienced any of those
   things?
   your brothers or sisters wanted to "kill" you
   you had to move to a new place when you didn't
       want to
   you were punished for something you didn't do
   other things that you didn't want to happen
4. Do you feel like saying something like this to God:
   If You really loved me, God, You wouldn't let this
   stuff happen to me.

Growing Together

When we enter the depression stage of grieving, it is natural to feel the way Joseph did about God's presence in our lives. During those times, it helps a lot to express those feelings directly to Him. Use the following activity to do just that.

Letters to God. If your family is working through a major change, expressing your feelings to God can be helpful. Have available stationery, envelopes, and pens (crayons for children who are too young to write). Then read Psalm 139:7–12 aloud to your family. Talk about how sometimes when we feel sad, we may feel like we are alone in the darkness, but God assures us that He is there. Then ask family members to write a letter expressing their feelings to God. Begin with, "Dear God, I feel sad today because . . ." (If you are not feeling sad today, begin with "Dear God, I feel sad when . . .") Younger children can draw pictures about something that is making them feel sad now or has made them feel sad at some time in the past.

When the letters are done, seal them in envelopes and set them aside. You can open them at a time when the grieving is over. They will serve as a reminder that God was indeed with you in the time of sadness.

CONVERSATION STARTERS

Each of us has different ways we react when going through the sadness of depression. We need to know what is best for ourselves and other members of our family dur-

Growing Together

ing those times so we can be sensitive to one another. Use the following questions to help all family members express their own needs during times of sadness and learn about the needs of other family members.

1. When you are feeling sad, what would you like others in our family to do for you?
   - ☐ Leave me alone.
   - ☐ Listen to me tell you about how I feel.
   - ☐ Give me lots of hugs.
   - ☐ Other: _____
2. When you are feeling sad, what is the best way for you to take care of yourself?
   - ☐ Do something quietly by myself in my room.
   - ☐ Watch TV.
   - ☐ Be with my friends.
   - ☐ Have a special treat, like a hot fudge sundae.
   - ☐ Other: _____

FAMILY NIGHT ACTIVITIES

DAB DAH Races. DAB DAH is an acrostic for the stages of the grieving process. Learning their names and putting them together with motions will firmly entrench the stages of the grieving process in the minds of family members and remind them that grieving is a process we all go through.

FAMILY ACTIVITIES

Growing Together

Teach the following motions to all family members. Repeat the names of the stages aloud as you do them. Remember to think "DAB DAH" to help you remember the order and names of the stages. When everyone can say them through quickly, have some competitions—both individual and team—to see who can say DAB DAH the fastest. Add to the fun by having small prizes for winners, being sure everyone ends up with something.

You might end your time by serving cupcakes with big letters on them arranged on a plate so they spell out DAB DAH.

D = Denial—shake head as if saying no

A = Anger—clench teeth and fists to make an angry look

B = Bargaining—rub thumb and forefingers together as if making a money deal

D = Depression—slump shoulders, arms down at sides, and look sad

A = Acceptance—raise arms to shoulder height, palms up

H = Hope—swing arms together and grasp hands in front of heart

Acceptance and Hope: There *Is* Life after Change!

GETTING READY

Say Hello to Your New Way of Life

In the first chapter of this book, we identified two aspects of managing changes successfully—grieving losses and adapting to a new way of life. The first four stages we looked at—denial, anger, bargaining, and depression—are all about grieving our losses; in effect, saying good-bye to that which we lost in the change. Entering the stages of acceptance and hope moves us beyond that point and begins the work of successfully adapting to our new way of life. To put it another way, having said good-bye by grieving the loss of our life as it was before the change, we are now ready to say hello to our new way of life by doing whatever is necessary to make that life good. Here are a few key points to remember about the stages of acceptance and hope.

Acceptance. We know we are moving into acceptance when we begin to feel that this change isn't so bad after all and that things could be okay. We still feel the losses of the change keenly, but we begin to experience the return of good feelings and, on occasion, even look forward to aspects of our new life. We hear ourselves saying something like this:

▶ I have periods of time now in which the sadness isn't there.

▸ I went to bed the other night and realized I hadn't thought about the divorce once all day.

▸ I know things are getting better; my appetite is back and I'm gaining weight!

In this stage we must remember that the good feelings return gradually. Our task is to welcome them when they come and not feel discouraged if we find ourselves feeling good one day and slipping back into depression the next.

Hope. This is the point at which the losses really begin to fade and our new life takes root. There is the return of a sense of anticipation and enjoyment in our lives, and an ability to see that there are good things about the way life is now. We can expedite this stage by embracing those good things and building on them. For example:

▸ Although I didn't want to move, this new house has some good qualities to it, and I'm enjoying making it into a home. Plus, the school system is much better here than it was in the old neighborhood.

▸ The divorce is awful, but I'm developing a closeness with my parents and siblings that I've never had before.

▸ I finally realized that if I'm going to make any friends here, I'm going to have to start inviting people over and making lunch dates, and I feel ready to do that now.

▸ I didn't want to go back to work, but I do enjoy the affirmation I get for doing my job well, and I've made several new friends.

And so, at last, we reach the end of the process. One last word of caution, however. Moving into acceptance and hope does *not* mean we no longer have problems to face or that we do not continue to miss what we have lost. Rather, it is the time in which we come to understand that change is a part of life, and successfully navigating through changes is possible. And the good news is, you *will* reach these stages. It *is* true that time passes and hurts heal. Or, as the popular saying goes, "The rain won't last forever."

For Reflection

1. List two significant changes from your past that are now behind you.

   a. _____

   b. _____

   For each change, identify the losses you grieved through and the good things that came from the change.

   a. Losses _____

Good things: _____

b. Losses: _____ _____

Good things: _____

2. Now identify a current change in your life.

_____

_____

What are the losses you are grieving and the good things that are coming (or are likely to come) as a result of this change?

Losses: _____

Good things: _____

3. What relationship do you see between questions 1 and 2?
   ☐ I seem to let the losses in my life overshadow the good aspects of the changes I encounter.
   ☐ I seem to want to skip the grieving part and try to make everything okay too quickly.
   ☐ It gives me hope that I can get through this current change as I did the past changes.
   ☐ Other: _____

Building on
God's Word

The stages of acceptance and hope are about moving into the future. Since we cannot see what is to come, it is often hard to trust that the future will be good again. And sometimes, when the changes in our lives feel too overwhelming, we can wonder whether God is really working on our behalf. At those times, the words of Jeremiah 29:11 are a tremendous source of comfort and hope.

"For I know the plans I have for you," declares the LORD, "plans to prosper you and not to harm you, plans to give you hope and a future."

If you are moving into acceptance and hope today, celebrate that God has taken you through a difficult change and is moving you into the future again. If you are still in the midst of your grief process, write this verse out and keep it close by. Claim it as loving words from our God Who loves you and is still at work in your life.

I Feel Happy Again!

Have you ever been in a place when it was raining so hard you had to cancel a party or picnic or something you were really looking forward to? You probably felt so disappointed that you wished the rain would go away forever! But then there came a time when you were *glad* for the rain. Maybe you were waiting for the rain to make your newly planted garden grow. Or maybe you can remember a time when a rainstorm broke a heat wave and made everyone feel relieved!

Changes can be like that for us. We may not like a change at the time it happens and for a while we feel angry and sad. But then we begin

to move into the last two stages of grief—
acceptance and hope—and we begin to feel that
this change is okay after all, and there are
actually some good things about it. You can
count on the fact that no matter how bad you
felt when the change first happened, there *will*
come a time when you will begin to feel better.
Here are some things you can do to help that
time come more quickly.

1. *Remember that feeling good about a
change happens a little at a time.* At first, you
may just have a few hours or one day of not feeling sad. That's okay! When you start to feel sad
again, say this sentence to yourself:

It's okay to feel sad again now because I
know I won't feel sad forever!

After a while, you will notice that good feelings start to come more often than sad feelings.

2. *You can enjoy the good things about your
new way of life.* No matter how hard a change
may be to get used to, each new change you face
will have some good things about it. Finding

Read·Along Pages

those things is an important part of getting over the change. For instance, can you see some good things in these changes?

▸ moving to a new place (you can make new friends; you might live in a nicer place)
▸ getting braces (you will have straighter teeth)
▸ your parents get divorced (there isn't any more fighting in your house; you might actually get to see your dad or mom more than before the divorce)
▸ the change you are going through

Now let's see how Rodney and Kacey are getting along with their changes.

> One of the good things for Rodney since his dad left is spending more time with his Uncle Jon. Uncle Jon is helping Rodney with a science project. Rodney says, "Wow, Uncle Jon, this is the best science project I ever made! You're coming to the fair with me, aren't you?" Uncle Jon says, "You bet!"

Draw Rodney and Uncle Jon.

Kacey finally feels ready to make some new friends in her new neighborhood. She's standing with her arms around two girls. She says, "I had fun today! Do you think your moms would let you sleep over at my house on Friday?"

Draw Kacey and her new friends.

There's an old phrase that says, "The rain won't last forever." It is one way to say that no matter how sad we feel, there will come a time when the sadness—just like the rain—will end. Draw a picture that will remind you that this is true. Above your picture write "The rain won't last forever."

Joseph learned about acceptance and hope, too. Here's what happened.

The Big Day!

If anyone ever had a reason to feel God had forgotten about him, it was me! The

days and weeks in prison dragged on longer and longer after the cupbearer said he would speak to Pharaoh for me and then didn t. I nally gave up asking the guards for news, and my depression grew deeper and deeper each day. All that time I felt like God had left me all alone.

Then one day the guard came to my door early in the morning.

Joseph! Wake up and come with me, quickly!

What? Go where . . . what s going on?

To see Pharaoh! The whole palace is in an uproar! It seems Pharaoh had a bad dream last night and he doesn t know what it means. He s been screaming at his advisors and wise men for an hour because they can t interpret it!

What does Pharaoh want with me?

The cupbearer nally came through, Joseph! He nally remembered how you interpreted his dream and he told Pharaoh about you. Pharaoh wants to see you *now!* Let s go!

I whispered a prayer to God all the time I was cleaning up and changing my clothes.

First I thanked Him for remembering me
nally! And then I asked Him for special
wisdom to interpret Pharaoh s dream. Then
I was ready to go before Pharaoh!

Lights ickered throughout the palace in
the darkness of the early morning. The
guard was right; the whole palace was
awake and thick with tension. I didn t know
what I d nd as I entered the room where
he was. The guard pushed me through the
door and whispered, Good luck! as he
closed the door behind me. And there I
was standing face to face with the most
powerful man in all of Egypt and boy, was
he upset!

It s about time you got here! he roared
without looking at me. What took you so
long? Oh, never mind! My cupbearer tells
me you can interpret the meaning of
dreams when they are told to you. Can you
interpret my dream?

Actually, I can t interpret dreams. But
God can. He will give you the meaning of
your dream. I hoped he couldn t hear the
shaking in my voice as I answered.

Pharaoh sighed as he started telling me the dreams that were the cause of so much tumult in the palace. Actually, there were two dreams. In the rst, I was standing at the Nile River when suddenly seven fat, sleek cows came out of it and started to eat the grass on the bank. Then, as I watched, seven more cows came out, only these were scrawny and lean and very ugly. I had never seen such ugly cows in all of Egypt! And then . . . those ugly cows *ate* the fat ones! I couldn t believe what I was seeing, and then I woke up.

He sat down as he continued. In my second dream I saw seven heads of grain growing on one stalk. They were ripe and full and good! Then, as I watched, seven more sprouted up, but these were withered and dying and no good for anything. Once again, the bad heads of grain *ate* the good ones! What does it mean, Joseph? None of my advisors can tell me!

There was such a look of desperation on Pharaoh s face, I actually felt sorry for him. I took a deep breath, whispered a prayer for God to tell me the meaning of

the dreams, and started talking. God is
sending a message to you, I heard myself
saying. The dreams are really the same
one. God is telling you what He is about to
do. The next seven years will be years of
plenty in which there will be lots of food in
Egypt. But after the seven years will come
seven terrible years of drought and no
food in Egypt. And when God says no
food, He means *no* food! The drought and
famine at that time will be greater than
any that has ever happened in Egypt
before. God has revealed this to you so
that you will have time to prepare.

Pharaoh looked at me with panic in his
eyes. Prepare? What do you mean? How do
I prepare for seven long years of no food in
our land?

My advice to you is to nd someone to
do this work for you. He must be wise and
good and someone you trust completely.
Tell him to make a plan to store as much
grain as possible during the seven good
years, so there will be food to eat during
the bad years. During the next seven years,
everyone must do as he says no questions

asked. His word will be the greatest in the land, except for yours, of course.

There was a long, long pause as Pharaoh considered my words. I held my breath, knowing that if he thought I was way off base, he would have me thrown back into prison, or worse yet, killed! Then he started to speak, and I couldn t believe what I was hearing! Joseph, the Spirit of God is in you! I couldn t nd anyone more wise than you! You will be my main man and I will tell all my people to do whatever you tell them! I will make it so today!

And he did! I was so excited! After all that time in jail, God was giving me more exciting things to do than I could *ever* have imagined! The long weeks and months of waiting had been hard, but now I could see that God had been taking care of me after all! I bounced down the hall as I got ready to begin my new life. I had *hope* again, and couldn t wait to get on with my new job!

To be continued . . .

Read·Along Pages

Remember . . .

You can enjoy the good things about your new way of life!

Remember, too, that no matter what happens in your life, God is with you and promises to lead you into a good future. Here is His promise to us:

I have good plans for you. I don't plan to hurt you. I plan to give you hope and a good future.

Jeremiah 29:11 ICB

Growing Together

BUILDING ON GOD'S WORD

Talk about Joseph. With your family gathered together, read the story of Joseph in the Talking Together section or read it directly from the Bible in Genesis 41:1–49. Then discuss the following questions:

1. What was Joseph feeling before he went to see Pharaoh? (depression)
2. How did he feel about God before going to see Pharaoh? (like God had forgotten about him)
3. How did he feel after seeing Pharaoh? (excited; he had hope again, and could see that God had not forgotten about him)
4. Can you think of a time you felt God had forgotten about you, but then things worked out after all?

Memorize Jeremiah 29:11. This verse is a powerful resource for facing times of difficult changes. Memorize it together as a family by writing the verse out on small cards (one or two words per card), mixing them up, and having family members put them in the correct order. Increase the involvement by making several sets of cards and having races to see who can do it the fastest. For a real challenge, review Proverbs 3:5–6 (see chapter 4) and then make up cards for these verses, mix them in with

Growing Together

Jeremiah 29:11, and let family members sort out both verses at once.

CONVERSATION STARTERS

Identifying the Six Stages. Read the following scenarios to family members and have them discuss which stage of grief is represented: denial, anger, bargaining, depression, acceptance, hope.

1. Josephine says, "You can ground me for three weeks instead of two if you'll just let me go to the party this weekend!"
2. Tina finishes all her homework for the first time since her parents got a divorce.
3. Louie screams at his little brother, "It's all your fault!"
4. Angel goes to her room and cries into her pillow.
5. Edgar is excited that his aunt and uncle are coming over to visit this Saturday.
6. Mary goes to her room and won't talk about the move her dad just told the family about.
7. Eddy goes to his room, gets out some paper and a black crayon, and scribbles black all over the page.
8. Ellie tells her best friend that she doesn't ever, ever, ever want to see her again.

Growing Together

9. After a whole month of not seeing her friends, Martha decides to play with them today after school.
10. George says to his dad, "If I promise to do all my chores and not yell at you and do better in school, will you move back?"
11. Joey says, "I don't care that I got a D on the math test!"
12. Bertha decides that having a baby sister is going to be a great thing after all!

(Answers: 1. Bargaining 2. Acceptance 3. Anger 4. Depression 5. Hope 6. Denial 7. Depression or Anger 8. Anger 9. Acceptance 10. Bargaining 11. Denial 12. Hope)

If your family is going through a change right now, take a moment to do personal inventories. Let each family member share which stage he or she is at and whether he or she needs anything from other family members.

FAMILY NIGHT ACTIVITIES

More DAB DAH Races. Review the names of the stages of grief and their motions from the last chapter. Engage your family in races again, as a way to reinforce the concepts of this book.

Looking Forward to the Future. Facing the future with hope involves both having events to look forward to in the near future and making plans for the distant future. Celebrate one or both with the following activities.

Plan a vacation or family outing. This is especially important if you are going through a difficult change. Having something that all family members can look forward to can help. Involve the whole family in deciding where to go, raising a little extra money for spending on the trip, and so forth.

"What do you want to be when you grow up?" Plan family events based on your children's answers to that question. For instance, if you have young children going through the stage of wanting to be firemen or policemen, you can arrange visits to firehouses and police stations. Officials at most facilities are happy to give kids a tour and talk with them. Other possibilities are visiting a hospital or airport, or having a teacher over for dinner. The main objective is to engage your children in thinking about—and celebrating—the possibilities of the future.

SUMMARY

Managing changes in our lives is not only possible but essential for living a healthy life. Here are a few key points to remember:

1. *Change is a natural, normal part of living in our world.* We will face changes throughout our lives, whether we want them or not. Accepting them as part of life instead of resisting them is the first step.
2. *Dealing with significant changes in our lives is a process of saying good-bye and hello.* We say good-bye by grieving the loss of our life as it was before the change happened and hello to our new way of life by doing whatever is necessary to make that life good.
3. *Everyone goes through the same six stages of grief when dealing with changes.* The six stages presented in this book describe a universal human process that is necessary to our emotional health. Each stage is important to go through for us to adjust to the change and move on.
4. *Bouncing in and out of the stages is normal.* Do not be discouraged if you find yourself moving from depression to anger, and acceptance to bargaining, and depression to denial. You will feel like you are

regressing when that happens, but you are *not*. Rather, each time you re-enter a stage it will have less intensity and last a shorter time than it did the time before. You *are* moving forward, and the process *will* end!

And above all else . . .

. . . remember that no matter what happens, God is with you each step of the way and He plans a good and hopeful future for you!

"For I know the plans I have for you," declares the LORD, "plans to prosper you and not to harm you, plans to give you hope and a future."
Jeremiah 29:11

Here's one final story from Joseph's life to emphasize this important truth.

Joseph Puts It All Together

I m an old man now, coming to the end of my life. As I look back on it all, the most exciting part of everything that happened to me came during those terrible years of drought that God had told Pharaoh about in his dreams. Oh, it was exciting to be Pharaoh s right-hand man for seven years. We worked hard during that time, and I was a ruthless slave driver. I know the people under me grumbled and didn t always believe the story about preparing for seven years of drought, but we pressed on. But, no, that was *not* the most exciting part of my journey.

The drought came right on schedule, just as God had said it would. It was terrible! No rain anywhere; nothing but scorching sun and dust. But we were okay because Pharaoh had taken God seriously and stuck to his determination to prepare for the hard times to come. Soon the drought spread to other parts of the world, too, and people began pouring into Egypt to ask for food from our storehouses. We had enough to share, and I began my new job as the governor responsible for controlling the sale of the grain. And then one day . . . it happened!

It started out just like any other day. I enjoyed meeting all the people from so many faraway places. Even though I had been in Egypt for so many years now, not a day went by that I didn t think about my home and my father and my brothers. I wondered how they were and what they were doing and whether my father was still alive. I was a foreigner in this land and so I welcomed other foreigners who came looking for food. But I never expected what happened on that day.

Next! I called out without looking up.

Your lord governor, please be gracious to us, I heard in a voice that caught my attention immediately. We ve come to buy grain. Our family is starving and we heard you are a kind and compassionate governor.

The attery was a common but unnecessary way to begin these requests. But this time I hung on every word. For here, standing in front of me, were ten of my eleven brothers. They were all here the very ones who threw me down the well meaning to kill me so long ago! I stood up and then I realized they did not recognize me! *Of course, Joseph,* I said to myself. *They have no idea what happened to you and certainly they are not expecting to find their long-lost brother as a governor in Egypt!* I cleared my throat and sat down. My mind raced as I thought about what to do.

Well, my heart was full of love and longing for my brothers, but you can be sure I was not going to let such a prime opportunity as this go by! I began to formulate a plan in my head and knew I would enjoy every moment. I haven t time to tell you all the details here, but you can read it for yourself in Genesis 41:56—46:7. For now, let me jump to the end of my story.

The day finally came when I could play my games no longer, and I did reveal myself to my brothers. It is a day I will never forget. They were all sitting at my table, still thinking I was the Egyptian governor and very frightened as to why all the things I had put them through had happened to *them!* Finally, I could contain myself no longer. Everyone clear the room! I shouted at the servants, and with great emotion I said to my brothers, Look! Don t you know me? I am Joseph, your brother! And then all the years of grieving broke loose and I cried so loudly the Egyptians heard me a long way off! At rst, my brothers didn t believe me! They crouched in their seats as the governor went crazy right before their eyes. Then I came closer, and called each one by name, and we had a reunion you would not believe!

And then, slowly, we began to put it all together. All that had happened in my life was really a part of God s plan! God had never abandoned me but planned to send me here to Egypt for this very purpose to save lives during the famine. Somehow, as I found myself comforted in my brothers arms, all the suffering and confusion made sense. I knew then that my brothers and father would come here, and we would live out our lives in the comfort of Egypt, together as a family once again. Never again would I have to wonder why all the events of my life happened as they did!

Yes, without question, that was the most exciting moment of my life, and I was at peace.

STAGES OF SKILL DEVELOPMENT

The key point to remember as you start using any of the family guides in this series is this:

**Learning new skills takes time
and feels uncomfortable at first!**

Remember when you were first learning to ride a bicycle or play a musical instrument or hit a baseball? It took time to perfect the skills you needed to accomplish those tasks, and much of that time was spent in boring practice sessions. You probably went through periods of discouragement and thought you would never improve. But persistence and practice eventually paid off, especially if the learning process was a group experience that took place in a friendly environment where everyone's efforts were treated with respect. It helped even more if you were guided by someone who had already mastered the skill and encouraged your every sign of progress.

Developing healthy life skills in a family setting is like that. Learning to live together in new ways will take time and commitment and patience on the part of every family member. Both you and your children will sometimes feel awkward and uncomfortable, as if things will never change for the better.

There are no shortcuts to making healthy life skills a reality in your home, but knowing what to expect can keep you going. Skill development normally occurs in five stages, as the following acrostic illustrates:

S = **Seeing the Need**
K = **Keeping On**
I = **Increasing Confidence**
L = **Letting Go**
L = **Living It**

S **Stage 1: Seeing the Need.** All change begins here. It is only when we are motivated by the need for change that we will go through the hard work of learning a new skill.

K **Stage 2: Keeping On.** This is the stage of greatest discouragement and the point at which many people give up. As you start practicing a new skill, it is natural to feel awkward, so you may want to revert to behavior patterns that are familiar and comfortable. At this point, you will need lots of encouragement and the determination to keep going.

I **Stage 3: Increasing Confidence.** Over time, you will begin to see changes, and the ability to use the new skill will take root. Learning to recognize and celebrate small steps of growth will build your confidence and keep you going.

■ **Stage 4: Letting Go.** As your skill level improves, more and more you will find yourself letting go of past behavior patterns and replacing them with the new and healthier ones.

■ **Stage 5: Living It.** In this last stage, the new skill has become so integrated into your life that it becomes almost automatic. When you find yourself using it easily, you realize that the hard work of the earlier stages has paid off!

APPENDIX B

RULES FOR FAMILY INTERACTION

It must be kept in mind that the family guides are only a tool to help you create times of learning and connectedness in your family. That cannot happen unless the books are used in an atmosphere of openness and safety for all family members. You can make your "growing together" conversations and your Family Night activities times of heart-to-heart sharing and fun for everyone by setting and consistently maintaining the following rules.

Family Rule #1: Every member will actively participate in all discussions and Family Nights. This lets everyone know that he or she is an important part of the family. Parents are expected to participate with their children, not sit on the sidelines and watch the action!

Family Rule #2: All members will show respect for one another's feelings. Modeling how to identify and talk about feelings is the best way to help your kids open up to you. Although you will need to use some discretion, letting your children know that you, too, feel a wide spectrum of feelings teaches them to acknowledge their own feelings and honor the feelings of others. If mutual respect is shown when discussing feelings, it encourages family members to feel safe enough to share openly. This rule means that no put-downs, name calling, hitting, or other destructive behaviors are allowed during family sharing times!

Family Rule #3: Everyone will speak only for themselves. In many families, one member often acts as the spokesperson for everyone else. This can be a child or a parent, but the result is the same. The other family members are not encouraged or even permitted to express their own feelings or opinions. You will need to carefully monitor your sharing times to be sure all family members feel free to openly share what they are thinking and feeling.

Special Note for Parents: Listen well! When asked what they most want from adults, children invariably report that they want to be listened to. Many parents unknowingly close off communication with their children by talking too much. Giving your children full attention and affirming what they are telling you will work wonders in building relationships with them.

Family Rule #4: No unsolicited advice will be given. A continuation of Rule #3, this rule is particularly important for parents whose communication style with their children tends to be one of lecturing or telling them what they should or should not do. Many parents see this as their primary role and do not realize that their well-intended instructions often close off communication with their children. In your sharing times, encourage all family members to replace such confrontational statements as "*you* should" or "If *you* would only" with "I" messages.

Of course, there will be times when your children do need guidance from you. If you sense that a child needs help, try giving permission to ask for it. "Would you like some help in thinking that through?" or "I'd be glad to help if you need help with that" is much more affirming to a child than "do it *my* way" messages. One word of caution: You must respect your child's right to say no to your offer of help. Hard as it may be to do, hold your advice until your child is ready to hear it.

Family Rule #5: It's okay to "pass." It is important to let all members know they can be active participants and still have times when they do not feel ready to share their deepest thoughts and feelings. Sometimes opening up may feel painful or threatening, and at those times family members need to have the freedom to pass. An environment is not "friendly" or safe if people fear being pressured to talk about things they are not yet ready to share openly.

Family Rule #6: It's okay to laugh and have fun together. In today's high-stress world, many families have lost the ability to simply enjoy being with each other. Give your family permission to use the suggested activities as occasions to laugh, play, and make a mess together. You will find that much significant sharing and relationship building happens when family members are relaxed and enjoying one another's company.

There may be other family rules you would like to include for your family. Just remember that the purpose of each rule is to assure an environment that is safe, growth producing, and enjoyable for everyone!